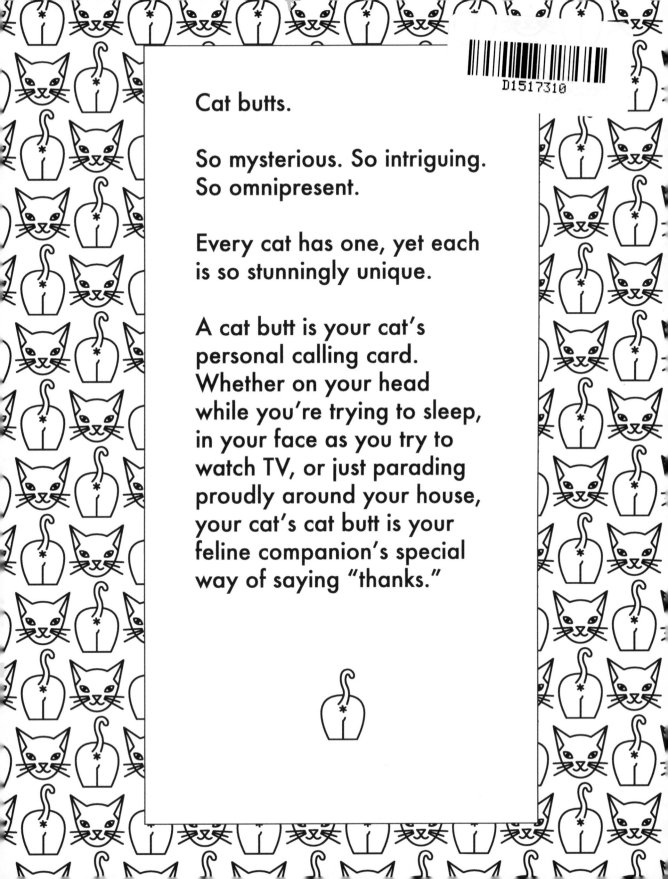

Cat butts.

So mysterious. So intriguing. So omnipresent.

Every cat has one, yet each is so stunningly unique.

A cat butt is your cat's personal calling card. Whether on your head while you're trying to sleep, in your face as you try to watch TV, or just parading proudly around your house, your cat's cat butt is your feline companion's special way of saying "thanks."

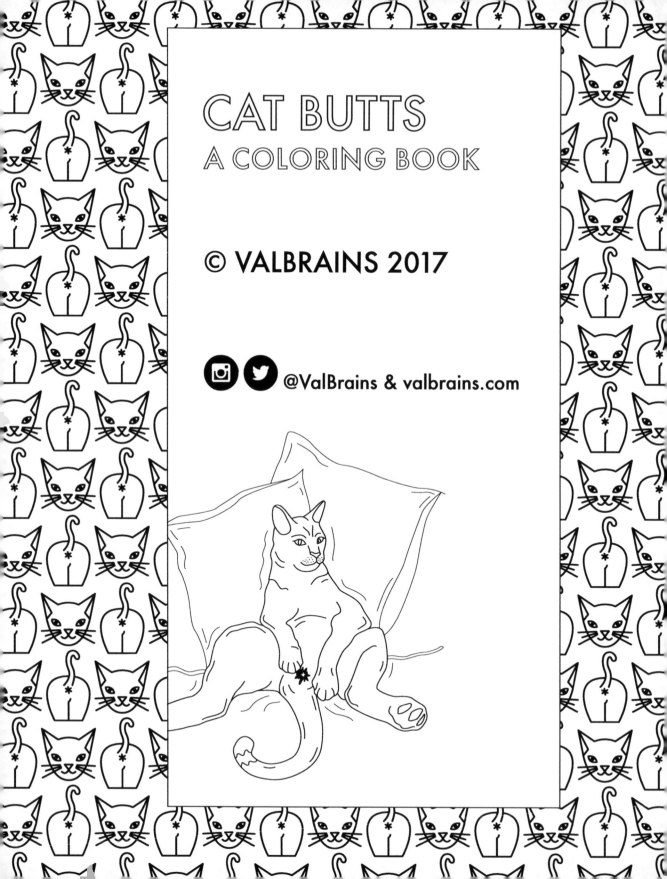

CAT BUTTS
A COLORING BOOK

© VALBRAINS 2017

@ValBrains & valbrains.com

CAT BUTT LOVE

fold down

To:

Colored by:

fold up

CAT BUTT LIKE AN EGYPTIAN

fold down

To:

Colored by:

fold up

FURROCIOUS CAT BUTT

fold down

To: Colored by:

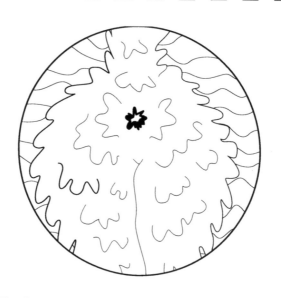

fold up

BETTER ON A SWEATER

fold down

To: Colored by:

fold up

THE EXHIBITIONIST

fold down

To: Colored by:

fold up

GARDEN VARIETY CAT BUTT

fold up

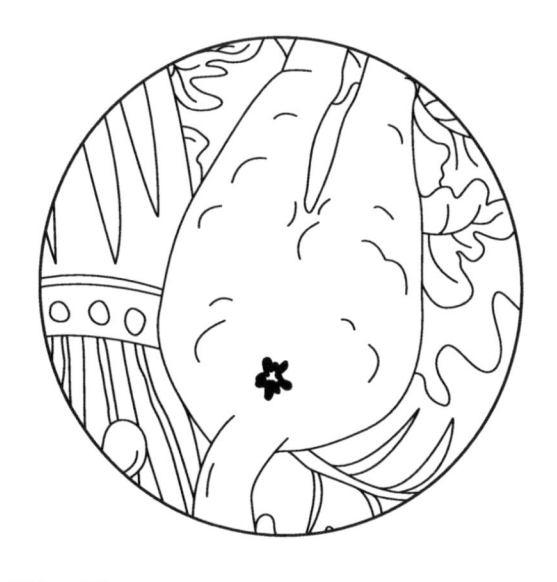

To:

Colored by:

fold down

WHAT ARE YOU LOOKING AT?

fold down

To:

Colored by:

fold up

CAT BUTT IN SPACE

fold down

To: Colored by:

fold up

RAINBOW SURPRISE!

fold down

To:

Colored by:

fold up

CACTUS CATMOUFLAGE

fold down

To:

Colored by:

fold up

CATBUTTMASTE

fold down

Colored by:

To:

fold up

HIPSTER CAT BUTT

fold down

Colored by:

To:

fold up

CAT BUTT IN THE WILD

fold down

To: Colored by:

fold up

YOUR NEXT HALLOWEEN

fold down

To:

Colored by:

fold up

THE SCREAM

fold down

To:

Colored by:

fold up

FOR POSTERIORITY

fold down

To:

Colored by:

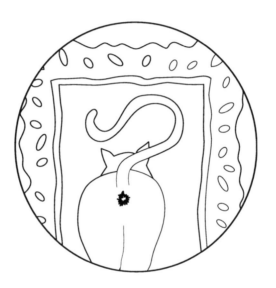

fold up

CAT BUTT CRYSTALS!

fold down

Colored by:

To:

fold up

CAT BUTT IN A BOX

fold down

To:

Colored by:

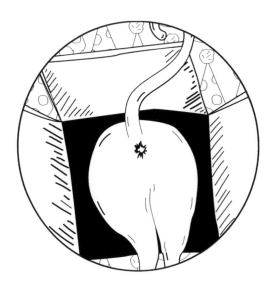

fold up

GOOD MORNING CAT BUTT

fold down

To: Colored by:

fold up

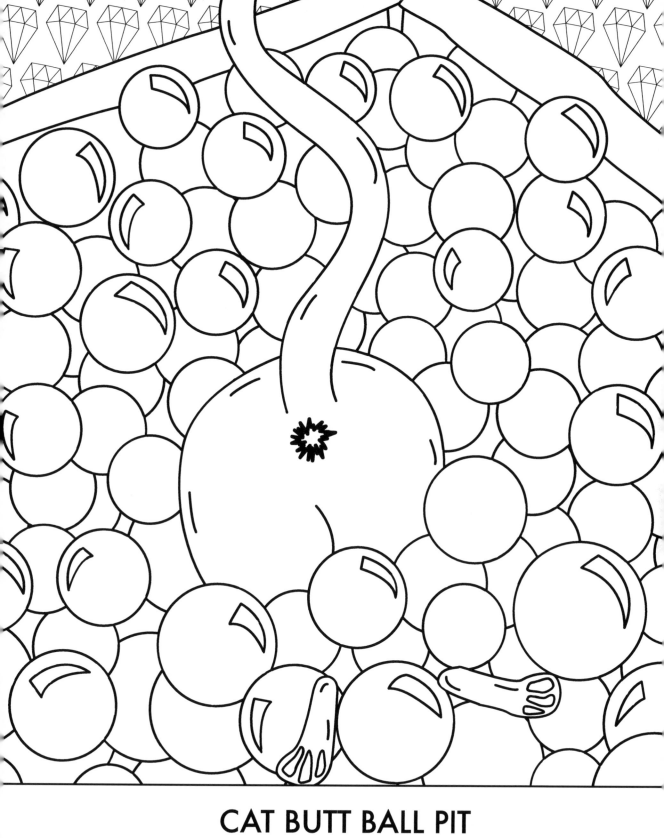

CAT BUTT BALL PIT

fold down

To:

Colored by:

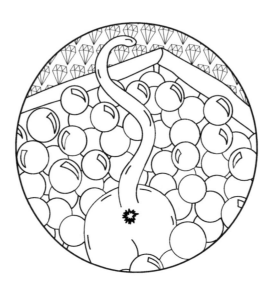

fold up

A CAT BUTT HAIKU

Cat butts in your face
In your house and everywhere
You are never safe

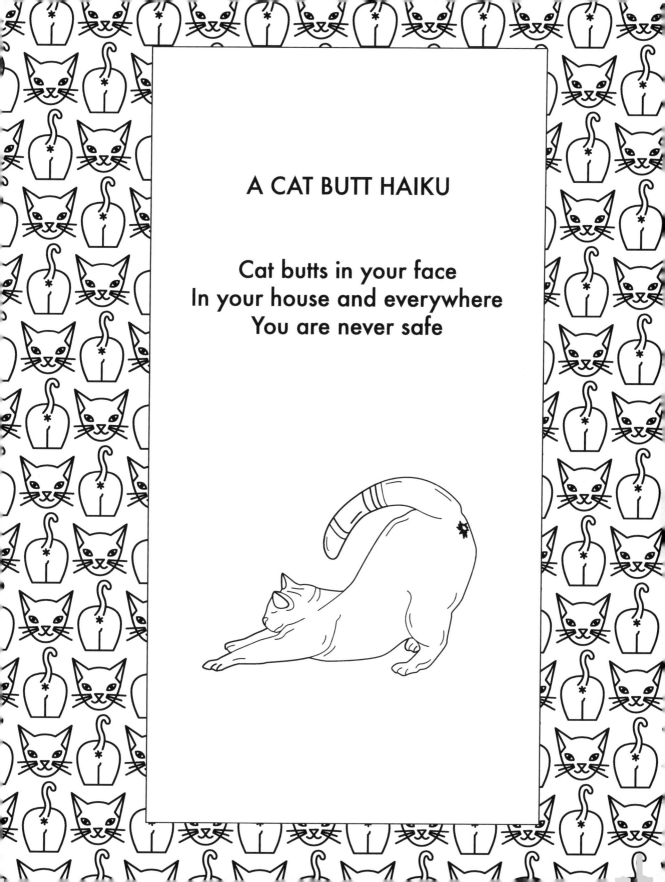

68837434R00027